EVERYDAY STEM

HOW SMARTPHONES WORK

ALICIA Z. KLEPEIS

Cavendish
Square

Published in 2019 by Cavendish Square Publishing, LLC
243 5th Avenue, Suite 136, New York, NY 10016

Copyright © 2019 by Cavendish Square Publishing, LLC

First Edition

Website: cavendishsq.com

This publication represents the opinions and views of the author based on his or her personal experience, knowledge, and research. The information in this book serves as a general guide only. The author and publisher have used their best efforts in preparing this book and disclaim liability rising directly or indirectly from the use and application of this book.

All websites were available and accurate when this book was sent to press.

Library of Congress Cataloging-in-Publication Data

Names: Klepeis, Alicia, 1971- author.
Title: How smartphones work / Alicia Z. Klepeis.
Description: New York : Cavendish Square, 2019. | Series: Everyday STEM |
Includes bibliographical references and index. |
Identifiers: LCCN 2017052585 (print) | LCCN 2017058765 (ebook) |
ISBN 9781502637550 (ebook) | ISBN 9781502637529 (library bound) |
ISBN 9781502637536 (pbk.) | ISBN 9781502637543 (6 pack)
Subjects: LCSH: Smartphones--Juvenile literature. | Cell phone systems--Juvenile literature.
Classification: LCC TK6564.4.C45 (ebook) | LCC TK6564.4.C45 K55 2019 (print)| DDC 004.167--dc23
LC record available at https://lccn.loc.gov/2017052585

Editorial Director: David McNamara
Editor: Meghan Lamb
Copy Editor: Nathan Heidelberger
Associate Art Director: Amy Greenan
Designer: Christina Shults
Production Coordinator: Karol Szymczuk
Photo Research: J8 Media

The photographs in this book are used by permission and through the courtesy of:
Cover Hero Images/Getty Images; p. 4 Kaewmanee jiangsihui/Shutterstock.com; p. 6 Science & Society Picture Library/Getty Images; p. 7 ©iStockphoto/Ardenvis; p. 10 ©iStockphoto/Mathisworks; p. 11 Tomasz Bidermann/Shutterstock.om; p. 13 A Moment In Time/Moment/Getty Images; p. 14 Stanislaw Mikulski/Shutterstock.com; p. 16 Santypan/Shutterstock.com; p. 17 John Stillwell/PA Images/Getty Images; p. 18 Bloomberg/Getty Images; p. 21 Andrii Symonenko/Shutterstock.com; p. 22 Rostislav Sedlacek/Shutterstock.com; p. 23 Maridav/Shutterstock.com; p. 24 Cburnett/Wikimedia Commons/File:ARMSoCBlockDiagram.svg/CC-SA-3.0; p. 25 Zhukov Oleg/Shutterstock.com; p. 26 StudioThreeDots/E+/Getty Images; p. 27 Chris So/Toronto Star/Getty Images.

Printed in the United States of America

CONTENTS

A young woman looks at her smartphone while charging it.

CHAPTER 1
UNDERSTANDING SMARTPHONES

It's 6:30 a.m. An alarm chimes loudly. A teenage girl rolls over and grabs her smartphone. She clicks on its touch screen. The noisy alarm goes quiet. Before getting out of bed, the girl sends a text message to her friend.

On the bus ride to school, the girl whips out her smartphone again. She quickly checks her email. Then, she plays Candy Crush. She puts her phone in her locker until lunch.

After school, the girl sits down at her desk with her smartphone. She looks at a social media app. She finds a video to help with her math homework. Before bed, she sets an alarm on her phone to wake her up tomorrow.

A Brief History of Phones

As we've just seen in the previous example, smartphones are amazing devices. They can do many tasks. But what are smartphones, actually?

In January 1878, inventor Alexander Graham Bell showed Queen Victoria how this early telephone worked.

Essentially, all cell phones are very small radios. Before smartphones, these early cell phones came in a variety of sizes, shapes, and colors.

To understand smartphones, it is helpful to understand earlier phones. Back in the 1800s, Alexander Graham Bell invented the world's first telephone. It used wires to transmit the caller's voice to the receiver of the phone call. This was the case well into the twentieth century.

Fast-forward to the cellular (or cell) phone era. Cell phones are wireless. The first cell phones just allowed people to talk. They did not have all the special features smartphones have today.

UNDERSTANDING SMARTPHONES

It may sound strange, but basically smartphones are very small **radios**. A radio is a device that changes sounds into radio waves that can travel through the air (or space or even solid objects). A smartphone or radio then changes these waves back into the sounds (like words or music) that we hear. Smartphones can also send and recieve words or images in the form of radio waves.

When someone makes a call on a smartphone, the phone sends a radio signal out from its **antenna**. This invisible signal travels to an antenna at the closest **base station**. Base stations are sometimes called cell towers.

The base station receives the radio signal. It sends the signal along to the receiving phone. Depending on where the receiver of the call is located, the signal might be transferred to a different base station.

Cell Phone Networks

Smartphones need access to cell phone networks to function. Cell phone networks are divided up into specific areas known as **cells**. A cell is simply the area surrounding a base station.

A city is divided into many small cells. Each cell has a tower. Every tower has electronic equipment and a big antenna. This equipment can both receive and send out radio signals.

As smartphone users move around, their phones switch cells. This allows people to keep up a conversation even while moving from place to place.

Buildings, vehicles, and cell towers are all connected as part of a local cell phone network.

FAST FACT

Cell phone carriers in New York City are competing for the chance to use light poles across the city as places to attach small cellular radio antennas.

Parts of a Smartphone

A smartphone is not just a very small radio. A smartphone is also a mini-computer. It has all the same parts as a full-sized computer.

The operating system (OS) is a smartphone's most important feature. It is what runs all the **hardware** and **software** on the phone. Hardware is the wiring and machines in the smartphone. Software is computer apps. These apps help you tell time, send messages, or check your email on your phone.

A cell tower sends and receives radio signals.

WHAT'S IN A SMARTPHONE?

Most smartphone owners know how to use their phones pretty well. But what are smartphones made of?

Smartphones contain quite a few different metals, including aluminum and copper. Gold, silver, and platinum may also be found inside. A smartphone might contain rare-earth metals. Most people have never heard of yttrium or terbium. And yet these unusual elements are used in smartphones. Many of the materials in smartphones are very hard to obtain.

Plastic is used in the casings of many smartphones. It is also in the liquid crystal display (LCD) where you see pictures and texts. Plastic is a cheap material to use. It's

The Kalgoorlie Super Pit gold mine is located in Western Australia. Gold is just one precious metal found in smartphones.

also pretty strong. Some newer smartphones have glass casings. But many users complain that they break or scratch too easily. Who knows what materials smartphones will be made of in the years to come?

The OS allows the smartphone to run different apps at the same time. It makes the computer inside the smartphone easy to use. Different types of smartphones have different operating systems. For example, iPhones use iOS. Samsung, LG, and many other smartphones use Android OS.

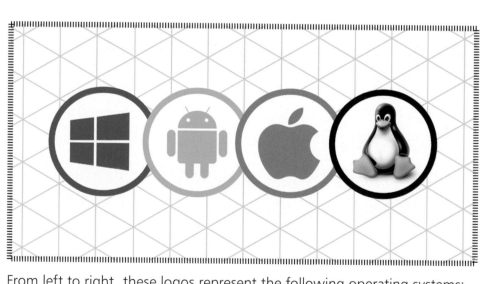

From left to right, these logos represent the following operating systems: Windows, Android OS, Apple iOS, and Linux.

Have you ever received a call while you were watching a video on your phone? Your phone went back to the video when the call was done, right? The OS made that possible.

A smartphone has many parts that play many different roles. It has a battery to power all its different parts. It has storage devices that help it work fast and save information. It even has a camera that takes high-quality pictures.

Wi-Fi

Many people use their smartphones outside their homes. They use them at cafés or libraries. These locations have Wi-Fi, or a wireless internet connection.

Smartphones can connect to Wi-Fi. But the user may have to enter a password to connect to a place's wireless network. A Wi-Fi signal typically only travels 150 feet (46 meters) indoors or 300 feet (92 m) outdoors.

This woman is using both a smartphone and a computer at a café. She is probably using the café's wireless network.

FAST FACT

Grand Haven, Michigan, became the first city in the United States to have citywide Wi-Fi. People have complete wireless access over the city's entire 6 square miles (15.5 square kilometers)—and also 15 miles (24 km) into Lake Michigan!

Who invented the smartphone? Most people assume that it was Steve Jobs or Apple. The first smartphone was actually made in 1992 by a company called IBM. The phone was named Simon.

Charlotte Connelly of the Science Museum in London holds up an IBM Simon smartphone.

Simon had a touch screen and software for checking email. This early smartphone also had a calculator, address book, and calendar. But Simon was big and heavy, weighing over 1 pound (0.45 kilograms). And it cost $1,100–pretty pricey for the time.

The Motorola DynaTAC was the first cell phone available for sale.

CHAPTER 2

HOW THE SMARTPHONE CAME TO BE

Fast. Lightweight. Multitaskers. Today's smartphones are all of these and more. But it wasn't always that way. Developing smartphones was challenging. There were many difficulties along the way. Let's take a look at the road to creating the smartphones of today!

Cell Phone + PDA = Smartphone

In April 1973, a Motorola employee named Martin Cooper made the world's first cell phone call. Ten years later, the Motorola DynaTAC 8000x became available to the public. It cost about $4,000 and weighed 1.75 pounds (0.8 kg). After only about thirty minutes of talk time, this phone's battery would die.

Fast-forward to the 1990s. Though cell phones started to be used more than landlines, they were only used to make calls.

What about people who wanted a portable device for storing information? They used personal digital assistants (PDAs). The Palm

Pilot was a popular PDA model. It had a touch screen. It also had built-in space for keeping information.

Cell phones and PDAs began to include email and message apps. Companies wanted to make an even better tool. They combined the technologies of cell phones and PDAs. The result was the first smartphone.

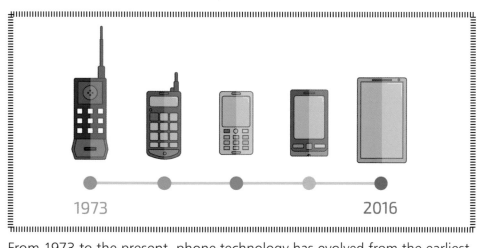

1973   2016

From 1973 to the present, phone technology has evolved from the earliest portable cell phones to our current modern-day smartphones.

Much has improved since the early days of smartphones. Their batteries last longer. Their touch screens are easy to use. Their cameras take excellent photos.

A man consults the GPS navigation feature on his smartphone while in his car.

Today's smartphones are equipped with GPS (global positioning system) technology. This allows us to easily get directions and let people know where we are.

DEVELOPING A SMALLER DEVICE

The first computers were so big they filled entire rooms! It was hard to create a phone that could hold a computer. Today's smartphones are filled with information. Yet they fit in the palm of a person's hand.

Nanotechnology is a field of technology focused on making incredibly small things. This field has led to many advances in smartphones. Inside a smartphone are many small components that allow users to store lots of information. Let's take a look inside a smartphone!

FAST FACT

In the future, nanotechnology may allow smartphone users to charge their batteries while walking, jogging, or doing other forms of physical activity.

The **central processing unit (CPU)** is the "brain" of a smartphone. For most smartphones today, the CPU is located on something called a system-on-a-chip (SoC). This chip is tiny. It can be as small as a shirt button.

The SoC contains all the needed parts to make the phone work. It includes the parts that store information. It also includes the parts that understand sounds and images.

The SoC is a great example of nanotechnology. Instead of having many

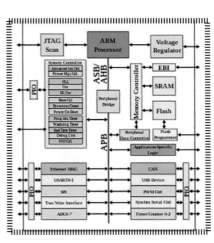

This diagram shows all the components that make up a system-on-a-chip (SoC).

separate parts that take up space, the SoC holds all of them in one place. Without these small chips, smartphones would have to be much bigger.

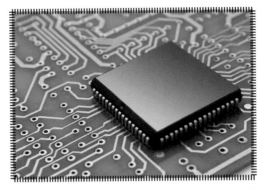

A chip sits on a circuit board. Wires will connect the chip to the board.

FAST FACT

The iPhone 6 can process 3.36 billion instructions per second. That means this phone can perform instructions 120 million times faster than the computers we used to get men to the moon back in 1969!

Smartphones have gotten smaller over time. So have the spaces where we store our videos and photos. Scientists are working to make them lighter and faster. They are developing batteries that last longer.

You can see the home screen in this transparent smartphone.

What will smartphones be like in five or ten years? Only the future will tell!

BE MY EYES

Smartphone apps connect people every day. The Be My Eyes app connects visually impaired or blind people with sighted helpers all over the world. How does it work? A person who cannot see asks for assistance in the app. Maybe they want to know the expiration date of the milk in the fridge. Or they need advice while navigating in a new area.

Tiana Knight uses BlindSquare, an app that helps blind people by saying aloud what's around them.

A sighted volunteer helper accepts the request for help. A video connection is established between the people. The volunteer can help with whatever task is needed.

TECHNOLOGY TIMELINE

1973 The world's first cellular phone call is made.

1992 The Simon Personal Communicator, the world's first smartphone, is created by IBM.

2007 The Apple iPhone is released.

2008 The first Anrdoid phone, the G1, is launched.

2013 The iPhone 5s is the first in the Apple line to include a fingerprint recognition system in the home button.

2017 Facial recognition technology allows users to unlock smartphones just by looking at them.

GLOSSARY

antenna A device for sending or receiving radio waves.

base station Another name for a cell tower that sends and receives radio signals.

cells The local areas covered by short-range transmitters in a cellular telephone system.

central processing unit (CPU) The part of a computer where operations are both controlled and executed.

hardware The wiring, machines, and other physical components of a computer.

nanotechnology A field of technology focused on making very small things.

radio A device that wirelessly sends or receives signals using electromagnetic waves, called radio waves.

software The programs that are used by a computer.

FIND OUT MORE

BOOKS

Amstutz, Lisa J. *Smartphones. (*How It Works). Mendota
Heights, MN: Focus Readers, 2017.

Everett, Reese. *Smartphones in Class, Yes or No. (*Seeing Both
Sides). Vero Beach, FL: Rourke Educational Media, 2016.

Stoller, Bryan Michael. *Smartphone Movie Maker.* Somerville,
MA: Candlewick, 2017.

WEBSITES

The Gadget Show: How Does Your Smartphone Work?

https://www.youtube.com/watch?v=u8Itn-MeZ7s

HowStuffWorks: How Smartphones Work

https://electronics.howstuffworks.com/smartphone.htm

INDEX

Page numbers in **boldface** are illustrations.

ABOUT THE AUTHOR

Alicia Klepeis began her career at the National Geographic Society. She is the author of numerous children's books, including *Trolls*, *Haunted Cemeteries Around the World*, and *A Time for Change*. Alicia's smartphone is an iPhone 6, and she enjoys picking funny ring tones for her family members.